The Paranoid Trader

An unapologetic strategy guide to retail trading.

By Sarel Oberholster

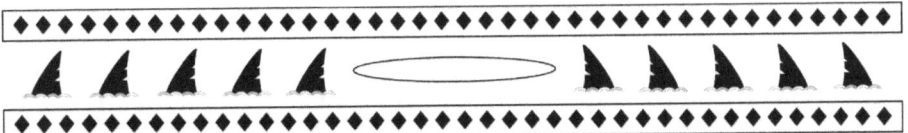

Copyright © 2021 Sarel Johannes Oberholster

All rights reserved

No part of this book may be reproduced, or stored in a retrieval system, or transmitted in any form or by any means, electronic, mechanical, photocopying, recording, or otherwise, without express written permission of the publisher.

ISBN: 9798543904527

Cover design by: Sarel Oberholster

CONTENTS

Copyright
Preface
Introduction

Chapter 1	1
We are prey.	2
Chapter 2	5
Get to know the traps.	6
Chapter 3	11
Find your winning style.	12
Chapter 4	15
The 10 Trades Rule.	16
Chapter 5	19
Arrogance is fatal.	20
Chapter 6	22
Maintain a narrow focus.	23
Chapter 7	27
Barnacle Trading.	28
Chapter 8	32
The 20%.	33
About The Author	35

PREFACE

This book is about sharing wisdom, strategy and market lore after more than 40 years of trading in the markets as a retail trader. Get to know the environment in which you aim to deploy your scarce capital. Understand the risks. Have a winning attitude, a profit-making objective and come to know the real market risks not taught in textbooks. Get to know the enemy in the markets. Get to know your own place in the market ecosystem.

Have you been making losses and need to understand why? Then this book is for you. Do you find conventional economic theory inappropriate for your retail trading activities? Then this book will offer you a new, alternative perspective based upon the real-life experience of a market survivor. Do you have all the tools for trading yet still fail often? Then this book will offer you answers and alternative strategic positioning.

All retail traders will find content of value in this book. It offers an overall winning market strategy, technical advice for successful trading and the avoidance of losses and personifies retail trading as only an old timer can offer. Keep it at your trading desk for you would want to be reminded often to deploy your money with winning strategies and to heed the warnings of danger.

Get to know the markets with a dash of satire, a drop (or two) of conspiracy theory and a generous helping of profit making and profit preserving advice. It's about you not only holding on to your capital but growing it successfully.

INTRODUCTION

I was working as a junior bank clerk in a mining town in 1980 when the gold price went manic. I had just started out, was dirt poor and had never invested in anything before. Stockbrokers visited the smaller towns on occasion, and it just so happened that one came around in the 2nd quarter of 1980 to solicit business from the bank's customers, as was the tradition. He was promoting gold stock investments. The gold price had peaked in February 1980 and was making a serious dip. I bought the sales pitch and went on using every last penny of my savings to buy the cheapest most marginal gold mining stocks I could find. That was all that I could afford. I did not realize or know at that stage that I was part of someone else's exit strategy.

The price of the mining company stocks fell fast but fortunately for me gold made another spike into September 1980 and the junk stocks went ballistic. I sold them all and realized enough profit for a down payment on a new, my first, bottom of the range, entry level car. I was hooked.

I had no method, was not fully aware of the risks and could only see potential profit. So, I continued to buy and sell penny stocks mostly making money not because I knew what I was doing but because I was buying in a period of high inflation during which all assets, even rubbish assets, kept pace with inflation. I even recklessly deployed my brother's university bursary payout in a technology company IPO which tripled in value and allowed him to cover all his costs, even living costs for that year. It all seemed so easy. I was so clever, yet the reality was that it was mostly fortuitous and plain luck. The losses arrived soon enough and only then did the real market lessons start. Enough losses and another Paranoid Trader was born.

The "market" is not a friendly place even when it looks very inviting and exciting. All successful traps look inviting, that's why there is cheese in a mousetrap. Cluster spiders leave the carcasses of their dead insect prey in the web to attract more flies.

The pain of losses brings a new focus to one's research, a new perspective. Look past the bright lights and the dancing girls and the market construct becomes visible. It is a huge trap. It has been designed, constructed, and perfected as a huge trap. The design has been evolved over decades, over centuries. It is still evolving, still getting better at doing what it is meant to do, to entice the participation of the unwary and to part them from their money. It is a brilliant design. Not meant to do a 100% fleece else there will not be a new flock to fleece. The "market" now consists of many platforms, many instruments to trade, many "asset classes" all spanning the globe. Its purpose is unchanged.

Sometimes you would get a warning, mostly you will not but this example is the reality (and probably understated).

> "CFDs are complex instruments and come with a high risk of losing money rapidly due to leverage. 71% of retail investor accounts lose money when trading CFDs with this provider. You should consider whether you understand how CFDs work, and whether you can afford to take the high risk of losing your money."
>
> IG Markets warning
>
> https://www.ig.com/za/client-homepage

The big trap is set, and it is populated by two main groups; predators and prey.

CHAPTER 1

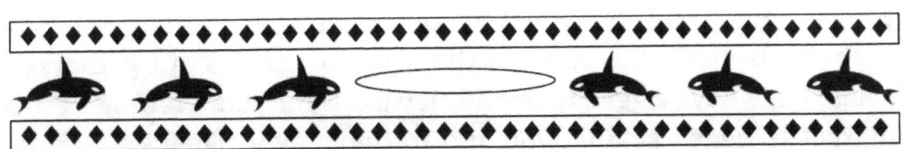

WE ARE PREY.

Your behavior will change once you come to understand that the market is structured like a food chain. You will come to understand how to manage your risk as is befitting prey. You will become more adept at survival. You will start to recognize the obvious traps and learn how to avoid them. You will develop an awareness of being hunted all the time. You will jump at shadows for they will represent real danger. You will become a Paranoid Trader. Successfully making this transition will catapult you out of the 80% prey pool into the 20% survivor pool. You will no longer be the easy prey but never forget even for a moment that you are indeed prey.

The market is a classic food chain structure with apex predators, predators, and a huge prey base. The predators span all predator classes from the ambush hunters like big cats to the mass harvesters like blue whales harvesting krill by the millions. You will need to learn how to recognize these predators and how to avoid your money being consumed by them. They have more resources at their disposal than you and they are the makers of the market rules. They have rigged many money traps for you. Trading in the market is rigged against you and in their favor. They know millions of little tricks to catch your money, to play your emotions, to manage your behavior and to corral your money for the feasting. Fear is a major weapon in their hands, and they wield it with ruthless efficiency as befits predators.

This market construct is brutal in its predatory nature. Even the prey will prey on each other. Just read the social media, the notice boards, the comments, or the platforms like Reddit. Your fellow prey is right there trying to influence your behavior in their favor. Some is laughably naïve. "This puppy is going to blow." "Rocket ships to the moon, baby." Some of it is loaded with confirmation bias factual information. All of it is meant to get you to support their market picks, to improve their chances of making money. They care nothing about your financial well-being.

Market Food Chain

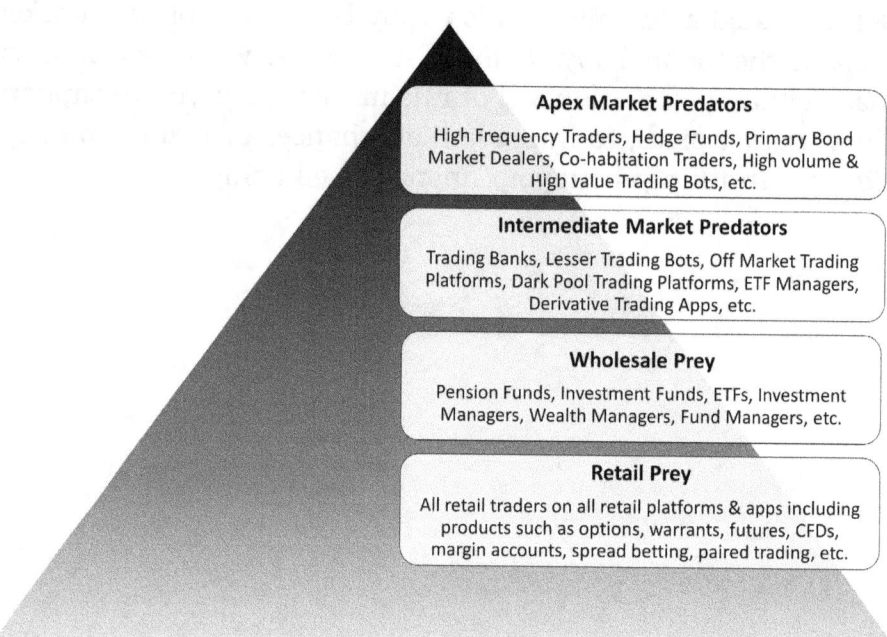

You will need to study the predators if you want to survive as prey. You will need to get to know their nature. You will need to recognize their presence in any trade. You will need to develop escape techniques if you are trapped in one of their schemes. You will need to learn when to run, when to hide, when to clam up to survive and when to seek sanctuary. By all means study your assets, study the trade, study the fundamentals, get to know the management, survey the prospects, run the models, follow the charts but you will get taken if you are not alert in your environment, if you fail to watch your back. Be a Paranoid Trader and know that the threats are very real. "They" are always hungry, are out to get you and we the retail traders are their prey…

CHAPTER 2

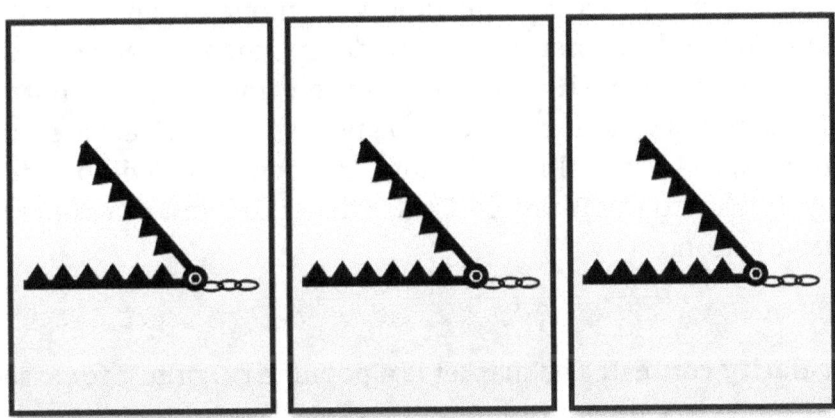

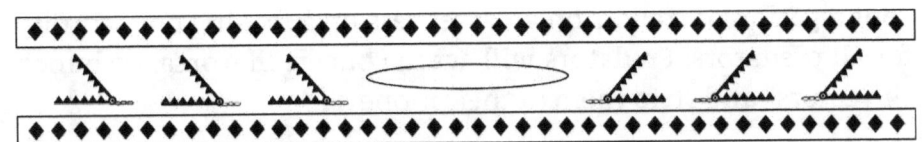

GET TO KNOW THE TRAPS.

Your emotions are the gateway to your money. Your greed will see you take excessive risks. Your enthusiasm will see you overtraded and vulnerable. Your impatience will see you rush into danger or exit a trade too early. Your fear will see you abandon your money. You are meant to work, make and save money then bring it to the market and transfer it to the predators, then go back to working and making fresh money to do the same again. Do not get trapped in this vicious cycle. Get to know the traps. Here are a few examples, the list is almost infinite and new traps will be added daily. It is up to the Paranoid Trader to get to know when to take evasive action.

Popularity contest: The market is a popularity contest for assets. Each wants to gain your money and they all compete for your attention, for your money, for your capital, for your savings. Each will accumulate a following. That is a trap. Too many followers will drive up the price and set up a harvesting opportunity. A huge congregation of traders on an asset sets up a feeding opportunity for all predators. Predators will act in concert like orcas to bunch "investors" and strip them of their money.

The narrative: The predators control the narrative. The media, social media and influencers will pick up the narrative and run with it until it is a crescendo. "Inflation fears dive down technology shares" is a narrative (inflation will generally inflate not deflate asset prices and particularly favor asset classes relying on capital appreciation such as technology shares). The move now is to "get out of growth stocks and buy cyclicals" is a narrative. Gold is in a primary shortage is a narrative (there is sufficient gold stored above ground to facilitate all manufacturing needs for many years). The narrative and especially the popular or populist narrative is a trap. Just read the disclaimers on research reports. It will often say that the publisher may do trades and act in a way which is in direct opposition to the content of the research report. They mean it. The Paranoid Trader must question everything. Narratives are for the ambush predators, nudging you to where the pride lies in wait.

Risk management tools: The predators will use language such as, your losses are due to you not practicing good risk management principles. It is a form of gaslighting. They will hunt your money and strip it from you by any means possible but will blame you for it. Use stop-losses you will be told, for example. Right, so you calculate a 5% down move should be where a stop-loss ought to be and set a 5% down stop-loss. Your stop-loss will be swept probably on the same day by the predators running the market down with an explicit purpose to trigger all stop-losses in a certain range and leave you with a 5% loss. Stop-loss sweeping is those inexplicable moves in the market which goes down by 5% to 10% in a short period and then fully recover. Watch them, they often end just below a round number, say a share trades at $86 dips to around $79 and bounces back to $86, all probably taking place within an hour or two. All the stop-losses congregating around $80 were "swept". Risk management tools and stop-loss sweeping are used by the hunt-you-down predatory packs.

Observation: Your every move in the market is recorded, analyzed, packaged, and sold to the predators. Usually, it is sold as reports providing "color" to market participants. It provides hunting information. How about knowing the extent of stop-losses at a certain price level, that would be extremely useful? How about information on pending orders (buy or sell) at a certain price level, again would be especially useful? Knowing the maximum pain level on option trades, that information is readily available. Much more harmful information is gathered such as information on leveraged trades, proximity to margin calls, distressed positions already on margin calls and many more vulnerable risk positions. That kind of information in the hands (claws) of predators means it's feeding time. Do not fool yourself, they do have that kind of information at their fingertips, they share it, and they act on it. Like shooting fish in a barrel or taking candy from kids as the sayings go. The Paranoid Trader must always be aware of his/her vulnerabilities and know that he/she is under observation all the time. Observation is for the silent killers like an owl taking a mouse. The mouse never even knew there was danger.

Controlled volatility: The predators control volatility. Economic theory holds that those who get newly created money first are the true beneficiaries of inflation while those who save in money deposits during bouts of money creation are the biggest losers. "Industrial scale" money creation has become standard economic procedure. Before 2007/8 it was used to inflate house prices and asset bubbles which popped in the great economic crises of 2007. The solution was to increase money creation exponentially and Quantitative Easing or massive money creation was born. New money is pumped into the markets by all central banks globally. Every year instability and volatility in the markets increase as a result of all the new and old money chasing assets. Flash crashes arrived just after the 2007/8 great economic crises and while a rarity and a reportable event in 2010, had become staple fare of the markets since then. Flash crashes and popular narratives often arrive hand-in-hand. Those who get their hands on the newly created money first and often, can generate the most value for themself. They also get the means to move the markets and control volatility. The quantum of money concentration with predators is raw pricing power and raw price manipulation power. Brutal power is the theme for controlled volatility, like a grizzly bear or a great white shark in action.

High Frequency Trading (HFT) techniques: It is no longer the conversation it used to be but HFT can fundamentally see the deal flow in advance and react to it faster than anyone else (lower latency). They can see who wants to sell and for how much and who wants to buy and for how much. They can then use that information to generate trades to take advantage. They can see you coming and will make you pay more if you want to buy and will make sure you get less when you want to sell. This reminds me of blue whales leisurely filter feeding on deal flow.

Co-habitation advantages: This started out as the preserve for HFT as they had to place their trading operations on the same premises as that of the exchange. Sharing a premises and connecting the hardware directly facilitated the almost zero latency requirements. The exchanges and the HFT collaborated to achieve that objective. Near zero latency is a vital component for efficient predatory behavior so all predators now arrange co-habitation privileges where they need it. Just stand back and view it from a retail trader perspective. Where does it leave you? Want to get to know the predators, see who has co-habitation on exchanges in place. Speed is the theme for these cheetah predators.

Deep pockets: Imagine yourself sitting at a poker table with players who have unlimited money to place bets and no limits on raising the ante. It will not matter how good a hand you have; you will always lose if a deep pockets can up the bidding until you run out of money to play. This is a reality of the market set-up. The predators can drive the market price to a point where you simply have to capitulate, especially if you are trading on leverage or on margin, no matter how good your trade is. This is an extremely useful trap. Corral a large number of traders/investors in a justifiably popular asset then fleece them by creating flash crashes using deep pockets, controlled narratives, high frequency trading techniques, co-habitation advantages and stop-loss sweeping while being fully informed all the time through real-time Big Data and Meta Data reporting. These are the nowhere to hide from predators. The hammerhead shark has built-in prey detecting electric pulse sensors in his head to "see" where prey is hiding. These deep pocket predators with access to data mining across all platforms have similar radar to detect and hunt retail traders.

The myths of the random walk theory, efficient market price discovery, level playing fields markets and other similar economic theories will be fatal to your financial health. The markets are not random and are better described as "shaped by predators based upon the popular narrative" with the only random elements remaining being unusual or unpredictable events. COVID-19's appearance is such an event, but it does not detract from the description that the markets are shaped rather than random. Just evaluating the examples of traps described above should make it impossible to describe the price formation on any asset in the markets as "efficient price discovery" or mostly "random walk". One would probably be better served by describing price discovery as boundary testing, price shaping. Describing markets as adhering to the principle of "level playing fields" must certainly be the most audacious statement. It is a playing field, yes, but it is steeply tilted towards the predators. You must be blind not to see all the systemic advantages handed to the predators.

CHAPTER 3

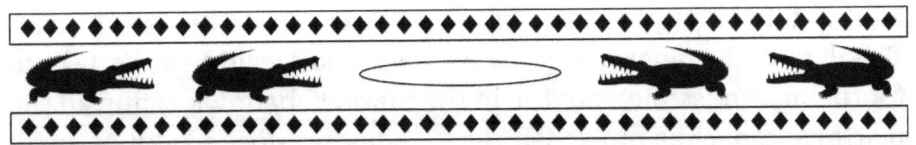

FIND YOUR WINNING STYLE.

The great Serengeti wildebeest migration takes place every year in mid-Africa. Herds of Serengeti's wildebeest, zebra, gazelle, eland and impala migrate to the Serengeti to feed on its lush vegetation after the first summer rains, usually around November. The migration in November is south and by May the herds make their way back North again, having overgrazed the Serengeti. The well-fed prey must cross two, now rain filled rivers on their way North, first the Grumeti River and then the Mara River, further north. Huge crocodiles lay in wait at the best spots all along these rivers for this crossing. It is an annual feast.

Predators study their prey, know their habits and seek the easiest low risk opportunities to feed. The predators in the markets do exactly the same. Herds of retail investors gathering and moving together will provide a great feast at choke points. The 80/20 rule applies. 80% will fall prey to predators. The Paranoid Trader will be aware and will take every precaution to avoid the 80% herd and to avoid the choke points. Do not cross where everybody is crossing and the predators lay in wait, cross at the unexpected. The Paranoid Trader is a ghost in the market leaving as little data footprint as possible, moving in the market shadows. Using all the platform tools like pre-scheduling trades, pre-loaded exit or entry points and stop-losses provide excellent predation data. The Paranoid Trader keeps sensitive decision making off the database and does not advertise his/her next move.

The absolute first rule of the Paranoid Trader is to avoid being in a vulnerable position. My personal sin is that I often over-trade which significantly inhibits my market agility and makes me easy sluggish prey. Hunting you becomes infinitely more difficult when you are fully agile in the markets and your behavior is unpredictable. Unique individuality will separate you from the predictable herd. Hide in the herd on your own terms but do not become part of the herd, the 80%. Do not be part of the herd when the culling begins.

The statement from IG Markets quoted in the introduction talks about "whether you can afford to take the high risk of losing your money". You will come across this type of comment very often. Another popular one is "never risk more than what you can afford to lose". I hear the sentiment, but I do not agree with the proposal. The capital of a retail trader is always precious, and one can never afford to lose any of it. The thought process should also not start out calculating "how much one can afford to lose". It sets one up for failure. Trade to profit, trade to win and hold all capital as too precious to lose. Yes, you will make losses but do not make it a state of mind and a precondition. Do not behave like a lamb being taken to the slaughter.

Retail Trading requires discipline and an individualized style of trading which will set you apart from the herd. No discipline and no trading method and you are just skinny dipping in a shark tank at night. You have to find your own customized trading style and you must refine it into a success recipe which will keep you in the 20% "too much trouble" group most of the time. Everybody gets taken sooner or later but you need to survive the encounters with predators suffering the least harm.

Most retail traders start out with economic fundamentals, even on a very basic level. I like that company because it produces software to protect against ransomware attacks, is an economic fundamentals approach. Economic fundamentals will probably feature in most trader's style and is one of the easiest ways to form a herd. Then the predators just need a narrative to create a choke point for feeding. So be ever vigilant when using economic fundamentals.

Next most popular style is probably technical trading and some form of charting. Again, these are crowded trading methods prone to herd behavior. Then there are quants, algorithms, trading models, Elliot wave and many more methods. The point is not to try and find the most obscure method, the objective is to find the method most suitable to your individual personality and style which works for you and yield consistent profits for you over the longer term. One which keeps you out of the claws and jaws of predators.

It follows that you should keep a record of every trade that you make. You should know why you made the trade and which method you used, and you must then evaluate each of the trades to see when, how and why you failed or succeeded. This is where the discipline matters. How will you know what works and what does not if you fail at this discipline? How will you even know if you are generally making profits or losses? Do this diligently and you will get to know your winning style and will then focus the discipline on keeping your trading activities within the bounds of your winning style. You will also know when to make adjustments to your style as nothing in the markets is static. You will have to constantly evolve with the market and your trading style must adapt accordingly. The overriding principle is still that you are prey, you are always on somebody's menu and you should avoid being vulnerable, easy prey.

CHAPTER 4

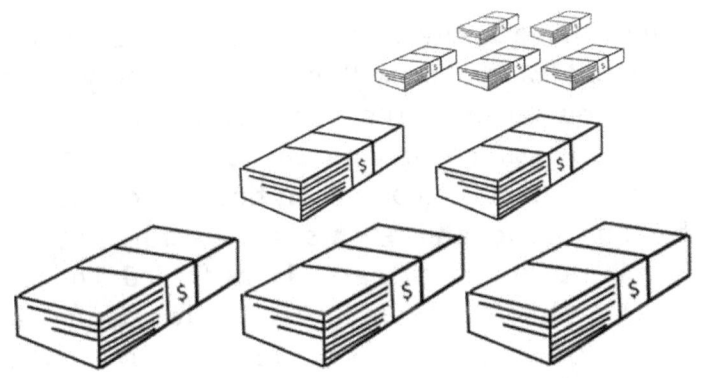

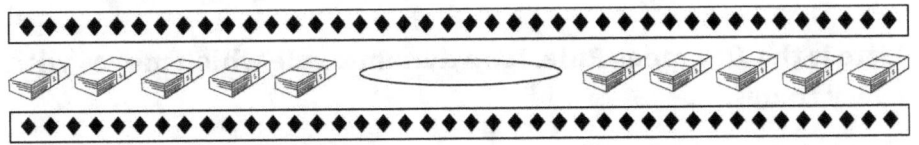

THE 10 TRADES RULE.

Google search the 10 rules of trading and you will find an almost infinite supply of 10 rules, and it is useful to read a number of them. The 10 trades rule is not another ten rules of trading guide.

The 10 trades rule acknowledges the reality of the markers and that of the retail trader. You will make losses and you will make losses often. You can have the best winning style method, yet the predators will still get you and the future is not known. Any moment in the markets can become influenced by previously unknown facts or events and "events" are even more pronounced when applicable to any specific asset being traded. The result usually is a loss. I personally hate losses, I hate making them and I hate how making them makes me feel. That is another of my personal vulnerabilities. It affects my market behavior. I have a tendency to cling to a losing position hoping for a recovery when I should be closing it, the earlier the better, and move on to more attractive opportunities. I have to guard against my hate for losses.

Here is the 10 Trades Rule. It's a dynamic rule which moves with every trade.

I will make a profit and be a successful trader if in the last 10 trades I had made 5 small losses, two break-evens or small profits and 3 big wins.

This rule tells me that 50% of my trades may be losses and 50% of my trades will hopefully be profits. The divergence which will make me successful is limiting losses and riding profits. That's the lesson but the 10 Trades Rule maintains my focus.

Keep losses small is the first element. This is an extremely difficult discipline to apply. I still fail at it often, but it does not distract me from the challenge to implement this objective. Big losses are drivers of behavior which encourage even more losses. You are in a hole and increase your risk profile to try and dig yourself out. This will hand you more losses more often than not. Clinging to a loss-making position at best ties up your capital and makes you a sitting duck prey for predators. Sometimes clinging is unavoidable and that will be dealt with in a later chapter but generally clinging will deepen a loss, perpetuate loss making behavior and deprive you of the ability to follow more viable opportunities. The first element of the 10 Trades Rule is to keep losses small. You must have the courage to make a small-loss decision (you have to be honest with yourself and admit a mistake) and the discipline to act.

The contrasting second part of the 10 Trades rule is to ride out a profitable trade but not to ride a profitable trade until it turns into a loss. Trade to make profits, trade to win. Use methods to maximize your profit taking. One method which works for me is to use a stop-loss as a profit taking tool. I will use a stop-loss at the exit point of a trade rather than to actually effect the trade once a trade reaches my target price objective (*Example below). It's hands on. I'll exit automatically should the price dip, but I will follow the price up with a tight stop-loss if it goes up and will keep following it up until I get knocked out by the stop-loss. I have often used this technique to gain an extra 1% to even 5% without being vulnerable or acting like prey. This is an almost no risk trading method (you could still get an unexpected deep fast crash) of managing profitability at the exit point. Develop as many as possible low risk trading strategies for both entry and exit points to achieve the objective of 3 big profits out of 10. Yes, do manage your entry and exit points as an extra 1% or 2% on both sides will add up over time to a huge additional profit.

The objective result of the 10 Trades Rule is that the first big profit be large enough to cover the 5 small losses, the 2nd big profit is insurance or jam, and the third big profit adds to capital. Nothing in the markets is so easy as to say that one can successfully apply a 10 Trades Rule without fail. That is not the ultimate objective of the 10 Trades Rule. The ultimate objective is to create a trading frame of reference and winning behavior within that trading frame of reference which will encourage profitable trading outcomes.

The 10 Trades rule is forgiving, pragmatic and achievable but hidden in the 10 Trades Rule is a disciplined capital compounding formula which will be wealth creating for those who can make the 10 Trades Rule their own no matter which trading method you follow as your personal style.

*Example how to exit a trade using a stop-loss. Let's say you have an exit price target of $100 and the price target is reached.

- Decide if there may be upward momentum left in the asset price, if high risk, rather exit directly.
- Enter a stop loss at around $99.75 or such level as you deem appropriate under circumstances. You can do this manually or with a tailing stop-loss. I'll continue to explain a manual hands-on approach.
- You may get knocked out at 99.75, then so be it, if not then follow the price action upwards, say in $0.50 increments. Thus, your stop-loss will be moved to $100.25 when the price reach 100.50.
- Keep following the price up until you get knocked out.

CHAPTER 5

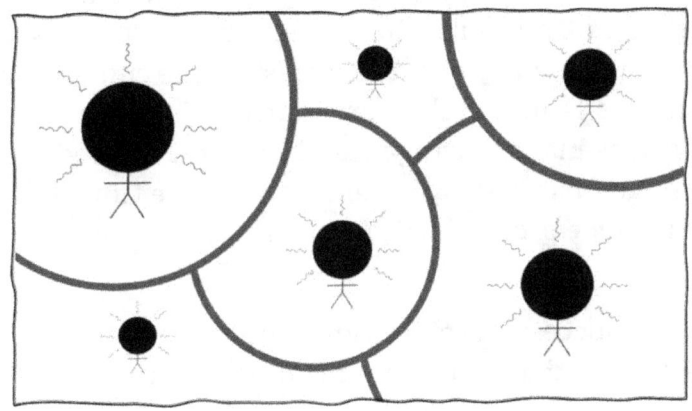

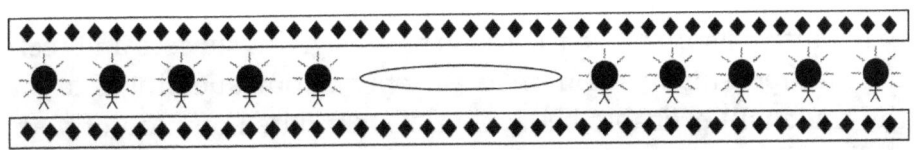

ARROGANCE IS FATAL.

This will be a short chapter, but it is a special chapter as it is probably the most important chapter in this book.

How many times have you concluded a spectacularly successful trade just to fail miserably in the next trade? Trading can lock you into a bipolar emotional rollercoaster. The culprit in an alternating success-failure cycle is arrogance. It is a guaranteed trade killer and loss-maker. Arrogance blinds you to predation. Your own self-belief has it that you are right all the time. Look at me, look at this huge profit I just made, I'm special, I'm a winner, I'm infallible…

Coming off a successful trade immediately makes you vulnerable. Own that! Know that you are more vulnerable to initiating a loss-making trade immediately after a successful trade and adjust your behavior accordingly. Develop a heightened awareness of risk immediately after making a profit. It would often be advantageous to give yourself a cool-down period after a very successful trade.

Arrogantly rushing into the next trade, high on success and feeling omnipotent, sets you up as easy prey. Your due diligence for the trade will probably be lacking. Your inflated opinion of your skills will see you taking risks outside the scope of your winning trading style. You will probably over-commit capital on a high risk "punt" rather than making a considered and measured trade. Arrogant prey is even easier than fat, lazy and incompetent prey.

Arrogance is not only a problem when you have just been successful. It is also a problem as soon as you reach a generally successful phase. It is also a problem of the ignorant. You must be brutally honest with yourself about arrogance. Evaluate yourself and every trade for arrogance. It should be a tick box for every trade. Does arrogance play a role in this trade? Do I rely on my gut (arrogance) for this trade? You can't manage your arrogance in trades if you are not prepared to acknowledge it and learn to recognize it. Go back to your previous losses and evaluate the role of arrogance in those trades. I confess, arrogance played a huge role in most of my worst losses. I'm ashamed to admit that I still have to manage arrogance as a high risk in every trade that I make. I'm equally ashamed to admit that arrogance still serves me losses.

Manage your arrogance in trades, for its long run trading implication will always be to destroy you as a trader. Yes, the Paranoid Trader is paranoid about arrogance when trading.

CHAPTER 6

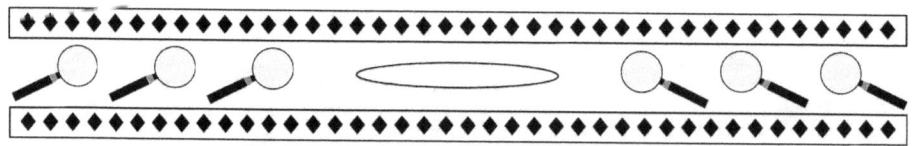

MAINTAIN A NARROW FOCUS.

You would have been told about diversification. Manage your risk through diversification is the textbook instruction. Do not put all your eggs in one basket is the saying.

Markets are difficult. Investing in any asset requires a due diligence. Studying an asset takes time. Becoming an expert on an asset is an almost full-time job. Just look at analysts. How often do you find that an analyst will only cover one company? How many times will you find an analyst covering 10 companies? They don't. Technical traders will try and argue that they can cover an almost infinite number of companies. You cannot. Every trade, every pattern, every decision takes time, takes resources, requires data, requires application, requires evaluation, etc. Even technical trading analysts will specialize.

The reality of the retail trader is, it is only me and myself. I do the trading. I make all the decisions. I do all the homework. I do the due diligence. I do the research. I follow every trade as I must decide when to enter and when to exit. When to book a loss or take a profit. When to run and when to cling. "I" does it all.

How many assets can you trade and cover as a single person in a market structured as a food chain, as a feeding scheme for predators? Every asset that you add splits your attention and focus. No analyst worth reading would cover 10 companies, but I have observed retail traders trading portfolios well in excess of 10 assets. One person cannot do the due diligence required to trade 10 assets simultaneously without cutting corners. Cutting corners is what predators hope for, what they rely upon for easy prey. Remember, your money will fall prey to predators, your objective is not to escape being prey, only to be part of the minority which is difficult or very difficult prey. Spreading yourself too thin across too many assets will set you up for losses. Cut one corner too many and there goes a predator with your money.

The Paranoid Trader is aware of the advantages of diversification but realize that it is in conflict with the due diligence demands of trading. It is not even a question of maintaining a balance. It is a choice; you have to mostly relinquish "diversification" and maintain a narrow focus as a retail trader. The alternative to a narrow focus is becoming easy prey because you simply lack the time and resources to manage the due diligence demands of a diverse portfolio of assets.

The retail trader will have to make conscious choices to specialize on many levels in every trading band. You must specialize on the basis of your unique talents, knowledge, personality traits, likes and dislikes, interests and everything pertaining to you as an individual. Next you have to specialize on trading methods and trading approaches, swing trading, technical trading, fundamental trading, momentum trading, day trading, trend trading, etc. Then you have to pick sectors and asset classes and eventually work your way down to specific assets. The idea is to keep the number of variables within a narrow focus and every sector will require sectorial due diligence, every method will add another layer of time and effort, every asset will have its own due diligence demands.

Stick with one method in one sector and one asset and your abilities will not be stretched. Add another asset in the same sector and your focus remains as one method, one sector but two assets for efficient management of time and resources. Add another method but keep the sector and number of assets constant and it improves your risk management. Add more sectors and add more assets and add more methods and very soon you are no longer in control of your trading, and you are just begging the predators to come and clean you out. All the *ands* add up and compound losses.

Case Study, my personalized trading style.

I have started out with fundamental trading as that is where I have a knack for trading successfully but in time found that timing my trades were often way off. Timing matters as it ties up scarce capital which could have been deployed profitably somewhere else and it often meant white-knuckling loss-making trades. I needed to address that shortcoming and developed personalized trading models to help me pick entry and exit points more efficiently. It took many years to succeed with that objective and "success" is only relative as there is no absolute recipe or model which will work perfectly all the time. I then had to marry the fundamental trading and the model trading which is an ongoing project.

This is how I make the trading choices applicable to my trading style. I use my personal preferences, knowledge base and personality traits to select potential sectors. The models do not work equally well on all assets so I test assets in those sectors for compatibility with my models and will eliminate all sectors where compatibility is poor while keeping sectors where compatibility is good. The result is a relatively narrow sector base.

I will then evaluate the assets inside a sector for compatibility with my models and select only those most compatible. I'll pick "to keep" only those where my models tend to be the most accurate, most consistently. This is not a once off process, I repeat the process in the down times when I have time available. Nothing is constant so I also keep track of the performance of each asset's model and eliminate an asset if the model fails to maintain an acceptable level of accuracy and profitability.

The result of this process is usually a "target portfolio" of about 100 assets which may be commodities or shares. The models are designed to be updated mostly daily but in need can be updated hourly for selected assets. The models are also designed to give buy and sell signals and to give some early warning of when a buy or sell signal may become imminent. I can't cover 100 assets with a comprehensive due diligence on each, but I can keep 100 models up to date daily, in need.

The next step is to identify any asset on a trading warning. I am a natural bull so I would very seldom trade a bear position. Thus, my trading warnings would mostly be an immanent entry point or an immanent exit point. I will shift to high focus and fundamental analysis on an asset with an immanent trading warning and do the required due diligence hopefully before a trade signal is given. I'll trade the asset if it passes both the model buy signal and a fundamentals due diligence.

I will maintain the process until I have a maximum of 5 trades in place. At that point I'll focus all my attention on those 5 trades and will just occasionally update the rest of the models as "background" information. I have found that I'm unable to do the standard of due diligence which keeps me from losses once I exceed 5 counters, so I'll never have more than 5 trades in place at any given point in time. You may have read some of my articles on assets which I have traded in the past. Writing an article on a promising asset is an excellent way to crystalize the "trading thesis" and to expose it to alternative points of view.

Every retail trader must develop their own style of trading and must find their own magic number of assets which they can cover without crossing the line to easy prey.

CHAPTER 7

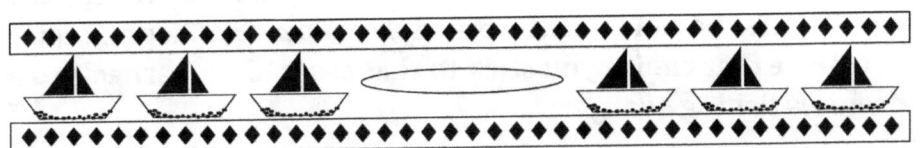

BARNACLE TRADING.

It is with some trepidation that I write this chapter. Let me explain "Barnacle Trading" before I get ahead of myself.

No trading method is perfect, and no amount of due diligence or foresight will allow you to make no mistakes. Often you will get your timing wrong, and you will be faced with trading out of an investment and risk getting your timing wrong twice more, trading out at the wrong price level and trading back in at the wrong price level. At other times you may come under attack from predators and will have to make a decision to tough it out or to fold. No matter what you do as a trader you will engage in Barnacle Trading at some point. Barnacle Trading is when you have entered into a trade and refuse to budge no matter what.

Ask any mariner about barnacles on the hull of a boat. Put on your protective clothing. Gather the high-pressure washers, scrapers, even acid and attack those barnacles. Do not allow them to dry. Getting rid of barnacles is a mission and getting rid of barnacles when they have dried is almost impossible without damaging the hull. That is the fundamental principle of Barnacle Trading. **Once you make that choice you stick to that asset like a barnacle to a deep-sea fishing boat.**

Clinging to any trade is usually harmful and clinging to a loss-making trade almost always ends badly. Why then would one ever engage in Barnacle Trading?

The first rule of Barnacle Trading is avoid doing it. The second rule is acknowledging that Barnacle Trading is a high-risk activity and must never be done unless absolutely unavoidable. The third rule about Barnacle Trading is that at the very least you must do it consciously. Engaging in Barnacle Trading without justifying it with solid research and unbiased information is reckless gambling and will probably end in tears. The fourth rule of Barnacle Trading is to close the position and take the loss, if any, when the trading thesis fails.

When would one engage in Barnacle Trading?

Extremely High Conviction Trades.

Sometimes in the process of completing a due diligence one uncovers an exceptional opportunity. Being naturally critical of any such opportunities the Paranoid Trader must make sure it is real and not a self-delusion. The risk reward relationship must be highly skewed in favor of reward and that reward must be material. These opportunities are usually tied to event risk. An example would be an opportunity in a technology company specializing in cloud risk management and increased cloud-based hacking or a pharmaceutical developer succeeding with a new pharmaceutical. You must be ahead of the pack in identifying the opportunity. You would enter the trade and hold on until the opportunity materialize or the trading thesis is disproved and that may well turn out to be a bumpy road. This type of high conviction trade can be very volatile as high reward trades usually are accompanied by high risk. It will also require a higher level of due diligence and ongoing research to ensure that the trading thesis remains valid. It may even at times require a balance of risks evaluation and significant subjective judgement but when these trades succeed, they succeed big. Just never deceive yourself about the risk. Knowing the risk will also guide the balance of your trading. It would be extremely foolish to trade all your trades as Barnacle trades. Predators will most certainly attack your barnacle trades and getting shaken out of a barnacle trade will hurt.

No change in fundamentals but under bear attack.

This may happen more often than we care to admit. It has become a feature of predatory behavior in all financial asset trading markets since 2007. It is also not unusual to find it happening as a result of a concentration of retail trades in an attractive asset. These are often vicious attacks which drive the share price much lower that you had ever expected, and a 50% fall is common. These attacks can last longer than you expect. That is the nature of the predatory bear trade. Hit the retail traders hard and squeeze them until they bleed. Build the fear levels in waterfall drops and shake the retail investors like a dog would an old rag. Shake them out of their positions. Rip the shares out of their accounts through fear mongering and driving the share price down. The only way this strategy can succeed, and it succeeds more often than not, is for the small traders to capitulate. Small traders in derivatives and margin accounts are even more vulnerable.

It is almost impossible to escape these attacks in time or to escape and get back in position at a lower level as the narrative and market moves are under the control of the bears. The fundamentals would also remain counter to the bear phase. These strategies are often implemented in the "after-market" or "pre-market" handing most retail traders the first leg of the attack as a fait accompli by the time the "market" opens for normal trading. Getting caught in one of these bear strategies is like having your head in a vice while the screw is being tightened until you bleed at the corners of your eyes. The objective is to get the retail trader to abandon the trade.

I have attempted escapes and returns with limited success. I often escape in time but re-enter too early or too late and end up making a trading loss on top of the trading costs. My personal success rate on holding out is better than my success rate at an escape and re-enter strategy. I have found it more profitable to learn how to manage Barnacle Trading when I'm caught in a bear vice than to try and profit from it but wish I had a trading style which would have allowed me to avoid the bear vice, or better yet, to profit from it.

It is extremely important to weigh the market action and information carefully. Holding out under bear attack and making a recovery based on sound due diligence and intensive research, works for me. Just holding out with "hope" as your only strategy will probably end in a huge loss and, returning to the 10 Trades Rule, I remind you that we must avoid large losses as it is extremely difficult to recover from such losses.

CHAPTER 8

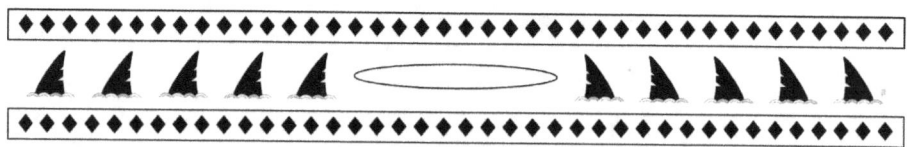

THE 20%.

The objective of this book is to give you a frame of reference to succeed at retail trading. The 20% does it. This is where you must make the decision. Do you run with the 80% or do you hide in the shadows with the 20%?

Are you going to be easy prey and hand over your money to the predators for the excitement of the markets and the thrill of trading or are you going totally feral, fighting tooth and nail for every penny? Losing money in the markets is easy. The clever structuring of the market will still reward you with the thrill of trading and the promise of riches while emptying your pockets. You will never see the "riches" while in the 80%.

The predators in the market prefer the easy prey and there is an abundance of those. Join the 20% difficult prey retail traders who are just too much trouble for the predators if you are serious about retail trading.

ABOUT THE AUTHOR

Sarel Johannes Oberholster

I have been trading in the retail market jungle for over 40 years. I have faced the consequences of every decision that I have made with no-one to blame but myself when things went wrong. I know the thrill of the win and the despair of a big loss. I have traded stocks, bonds, derivatives, hard commodities and soft commodities across global platforms. I do my own due diligence and always take full responsibility for every trading decision that I make.

I am trained as an economist. Writing was something I turned to in 2004 when I became aware of the potential for a systemic market event as a result of excessive money creation. I wrote a number of articles in which I accurately described how the economic systemic event would unfold. I explained how the spark would come from an interbank meltdown and spiral out of control across the banking sector, the financial sector and the markets.

I have published a scientific paper in the aftermath of the 2007/9 Global Financial Crises, "War on Savings", in the Journal of Financial Regulation and Compliance (Emerald Group Publishing Limited, partner of the Thompson Reuters Group). I am a Literati Network Member of Emerald.

I have published more than 70 articles across a number of publishers and lately have been publishing exclusively on Seeking Alpha. This is my first attempt at writing a book and I wanted to share some of the strategic knowledge that I have gained over decades of trading in an easily digestible format. I wish every retail trader only the best of luck and the courage to make good decisions. May you always grow your capital.

RETAIL TRADER GUIDES

The books in this series are designed to guide the Retail Trader to protect his capital before attempting to grow his capital. The Retail Trader plays defense and is too small to play offense. Learn to play defense well and you will become a successful Retail Trader. Ignore defense and you may as well just spend your money for, in the market, it will be taken from you.

The first book in the series is The Paranoid Trader and the second book in the series is The BIG FISH Trader. Keep them at your trading station for you will want to refer back to them form time to time.

The Paranoid Trader

Have you ever been perplexed as a Retail Trader or Retail Investor about the disconnect between economic fundamentals and the share price of a company or asset? Have you sold your assets or shares as a Retail Trader in despair because the price just keeps falling, just to see the price bottoming a week or two later and proceed to make new all time highs soon after, actually proving your investment thesis right, yet you still ended with a loss? Do you want to know why?

The Big Fish Trader

The BIG FISH Trader is that trader who swims past your trading account and swallows it whole. It's gone. Meet and greet the BIG FISH trader and check whether your fingers are still attached to your hand. No, you know what, check whether your arm is still attached to your body!

Get to know the BIG FISH trader and learn how to play defense effectively. Know your trading environment and protect your capital. Only after you have learned how to hold on to your capital will you succeed in growing your capital.

www.ingramcontent.com/pod-product-compliance
Lightning Source LLC
Chambersburg PA
CBHW070841220526
45466CB00002B/849